EARTH FILES

MOUNTAINS

EARTH FILES – MOUNTAINS
was produced by

David West ☆☆ **Children's Books**

7 Princeton Court
55 Felsham Road
London SW15 1AZ

Editor: James Pickering
Picture Research: Carrie Haines

First published in Great Britain in 2002 by
Heinemann Library, Halley Court, Jordan Hill,
Oxford OX2 8EJ, a division of Reed Educational and
Professional Publishing Limited.

OXFORD MELBOURNE AUCKLAND
JOHANNESBURG BLANTYRE GABORONE
IBADAN PORTSMOUTH (NH) USA CHICAGO

Copyright © 2002 David West Children's Books

06 05 04 03 02
10 9 8 7 6 5 4 3 2 1

ISBN 0 431 15621 2 (HB)
ISBN 0 431 15628 X (PB)

British Library Cataloguing in Publication Data

Oxlade, Chris
Mountains. - (Earth Files)
1. Mountains - Juvenile literature
2. Mountain ecology - Juvenile literature
I. Title
551.4'32

PHOTO CREDITS :
Abbreviations: t-top, m-middle, b-bottom, r-right,
l-left, c-centre.

Front cover, 3, 4t & 25tl, 4-5b, 5t & 7br, 5b, 6-7b, 8
both, 12ml & br, 13 all, 14-15t, 15tr, 16 all, 18bl,
18-19b, 20 all, 21br & mr, 22bl, 26-27r, 28bl, 28-
29t, 29 both - Corbis Images. 9tl - Roger Vlitos. 10tr
(E Mickleburgh), 11tl (François Gohier), 21tl (Jean-
Paul Ferrero), 21tr (McDougal Tiger Tops), 21bl
(Stefan Meyers), 27b (D. et S. Simon) - Ardea Londor
Ltd. 10-11b (Raj Kamal), 17tl (Bildagentur
Schuster/D.R.), 18ml (F. Jackson), 18mr (Bildagentur
Schuster/Mallaun), 19bl (Ama Dablam), 20-21
(Walter Rawlings), 23tl (N.A. Callow), 23tm (Geoff
Renner), 24bl (Sassoon), 25mr (Gavin Hellier), 9mr,
12tr, 15b, 22tr, 23br, 24tr, 24-25b, 27mr - Robert
Harding Picture Library. 14ml, 17mr, 27tl -
Popperfoto/Reuters. 19br - R.G.S. and Alpine
Club/John Frost Newspapers.

Printed and bound in Italy

*An explanation of difficult words can be
found in the glossary on page 31.*

EARTH FILES

MOUNTAINS

Chris Oxlade

Heinemann LIBRARY

CONTENTS

Millions of people live and work in mountainous regions of the world. These local Indians live high in the Andes in Ecuador.

Steep-sided mountains attract skiers, hikers and mountaineer. But they can be dangerous places, with frequent bad weather and avalanches.

INTRODUCTION

Towering mountains, with jagged or snow-capped peaks, are a feature of every continent on Earth. In fact, mountains cover nearly a quarter of the Earth's surface. Spectacular mountain chains stretch the length of whole continents, vast volcanoes spring out of the countryside, and huge undersea mountains cover the sea bed. The mountains are homes to plants, animals and people. They have found ways of surviving in the harsh high-altitude environment of the mountain tops.

In some parts of the world molten rock from deep underground escapes to the surface. It piles up into cone-shaped volcanoes.

Animals such as this Bighorn sheep are adapted for a life in the mountains. The Bighorn has a thick, coarse coat to keep out the biting wind and cold.

Some mountains stand on their own, but most are in huge groups called mountain ranges. Ranges join together to form mountain systems. The biggest systems are the Himalayas, the Rocky Mountains and the Andes.

MOUNTAIN HEIGHTS

Mountain heights are measured in metres from sea level (even though mountains can be thousands of kilometres from the sea). In general, hills more than 1,000 metres high are called mountains. A high mountain in one country might only rank as a small one in another.

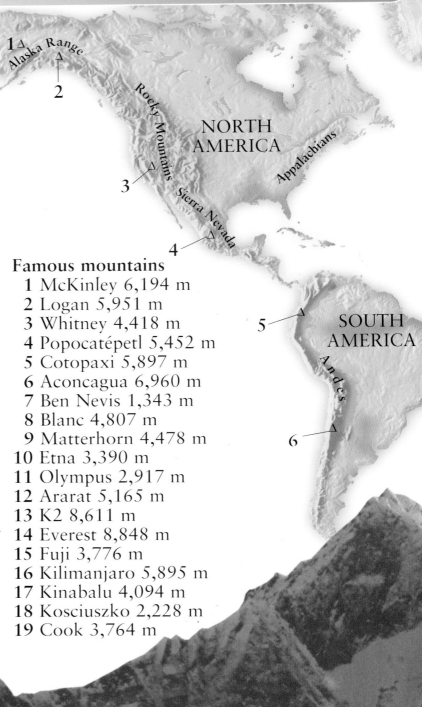

Famous mountains
1 McKinley 6,194 m
2 Logan 5,951 m
3 Whitney 4,418 m
4 Popocatépetl 5,452 m
5 Cotopaxi 5,897 m
6 Aconcagua 6,960 m
7 Ben Nevis 1,343 m
8 Blanc 4,807 m
9 Matterhorn 4,478 m
10 Etna 3,390 m
11 Olympus 2,917 m
12 Ararat 5,165 m
13 K2 8,611 m
14 Everest 8,848 m
15 Fuji 3,776 m
16 Kilimanjaro 5,895 m
17 Kinabalu 4,094 m
18 Kosciuszko 2,228 m
19 Cook 3,764 m

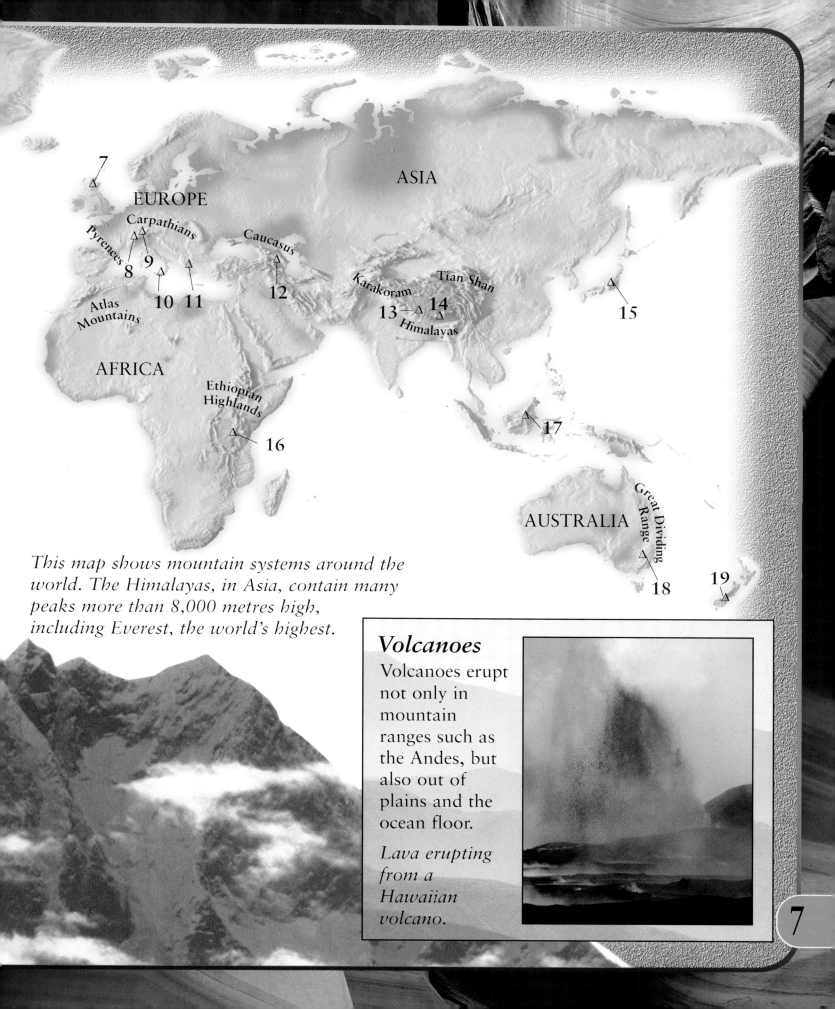

ASIA

EUROPE

7

Carpathians

Pyrenees

Caucasus

Tian Shan

Karakoram

8   9

10 11

12

13 → 14

Himalayas

Atlas
Mountains

15

AFRICA

Ethiopian
Highlands

16

17

AUSTRALIA

Great Dividing Range

18

19

This map shows mountain systems around the world. The Himalayas, in Asia, contain many peaks more than 8,000 metres high, including Everest, the world's highest.

Volcanoes

Volcanoes erupt not only in mountain ranges such as the Andes, but also out of plains and the ocean floor.

Lava erupting from a Hawaiian volcano.

MAKING MOUNTAINS

The Earth's rocky, outer layer is called the crust. Mountains are formed over millions of years as movements in the crust make the layers of rock fold, crack, and lift up. Sometimes mountains are made by volcanic activity.

TYPES OF MOUNTAIN

Geologists divide mountains into four types. They are fold mountains, block mountains, dome mountains and volcanoes. Each is named after the way it is made. Most mountains, including the Himalayas, the Alps and the Rocky Mountains, are fold mountains. The Earth's crust is divided into several huge slabs called tectonic plates, which drift slowly on the soft rock beneath. Fold mountains are made where two plates crash into each other.

FOLDING ROCKS

Where two tectonic plates move towards each other, one plate may slide under the other. This is called a subduction zone. Layers of rocks near the surface are scrunched together, and the immense forces buckle and fold the layers into mountains. The Himalayas were pushed up when India crashed into the rest of Asia about 50 million years ago. Layers of rocks on the bed of an ancient ocean were squashed between the two pieces of continental crust, forced upwards, bent and cracked to form the jagged Himalayas.

The Himalayas from space. These are fold mountains.

The Rocky Mountains were formed as the continent of North America crashed into the enormous Pacific tectonic plate.

These twisted layers of sandstone in New Mexico, USA, were flat and horizontal when they were part of an ancient sea bed.

Fish in the mountains

Fold mountains are sometimes made from sedimentary rocks that were part of the ancient sea bed. These rocks often contain fossils of sea creatures. This is why fossils of sea creatures such as ammonites have been found thousands of metres up in the mountains.

Ammonite fossils.

Continents move towards each other

Ancient ocean

Continental crust

Oceanic crust

Layers of rock buckle and fold to form mountains

Continents join together

9

Block mountains are formed when the Earth's crust cracks into huge blocks, and the blocks rise or fall. Dome mountains are formed when molten rock pushes the crust upwards.

BREAKING ROCKS

Enormous forces are created as the tectonic plates of the Earth's crust slide into each other or past each other. These forces can cause the layers of rock in the crust to crack into the blocks that form block mountains.

MOLTEN MAGMA

The thickness of the Earth's crust varies from about 5 kilometres to about 90 kilometres. Beneath the crust is a layer of extremely hot, molten rock, called magma. Magma is responsible for making dome mountains.

The Great Rift Valley

Sometimes blocks slip down instead of up. A falling block forms a valley called a rift valley, with mountains on either side. The Great Rift Valley stretches nearly 5,000 kilometres through Africa. In places it is 160 kilometres wide.

The Great Rift Valley.

The Langdale Fells are hills in England's Lake District. All the mountains in this area are ancient dome mountains.

MAKING BLOCK AND DOME MOUNTAINS

The cracks in the Earth's crust are called faults. They can extend many kilometres into the crust. Pressure from above or from the sides forces rocks on either side of a fault to slide past each other. If a block between two faults moves upwards, it forms a flat-topped mountain range.

Block mountain

Fault   Block forced up   Fault

If there is a weak spot in the crust, magma moves upwards. When a huge mass of magma rises, it pushes up the layers of rock above it, forming a bulge called a dome mountain.

Mount Rundle in Banff National Park, Canada. You can see the layers of rock that have been forced upwards to form this sheer-sided, flat-topped block mountain.

Dome mountain   Crust forced up

Magma dome

11

Volcanoes are places where molten rock called magma leaks out through the Earth's crust and builds mountains. Most volcanoes form along the edges of tectonic plates, where the plates crash together or split apart.

Puy de Dôme, France, is an extinct volcano. 'Extinct' means that it has not erupted for a very long time, and will probably never erupt again.

Cotopaxi, an active volcano in the Andes in Ecuador.

VOLCANO TYPES

Gentle eruptions happen where the magma is thin and runny. It flows out, runs quickly down the volcano's sides and then sets. Gentle eruptions form volcanoes that are wide and low, called shield volcanoes. Violent eruptions happen when thick magma full of gas builds up inside a volcano and then bursts out explosively, creating clouds of ash, dust and gas. Violent eruptions form cone-shaped volcanoes.

The spectacular Devil's Tower in Wyoming, USA, is a volcanic plug. Its thin columns were formed as the magma cooled and cracked inside the volcano.

VOLCANO PARTS

Volcanoes form where magma wells up to create a magma reservoir a few kilometres underground, and then breaks through to the surface. When magma reaches the surface it is known as lava. Layers of ash and lava from eruptions build up a cone-shaped mountain, with pipes called conduits inside that carry magma to vents. A hollow crater forms at the top of the cone.

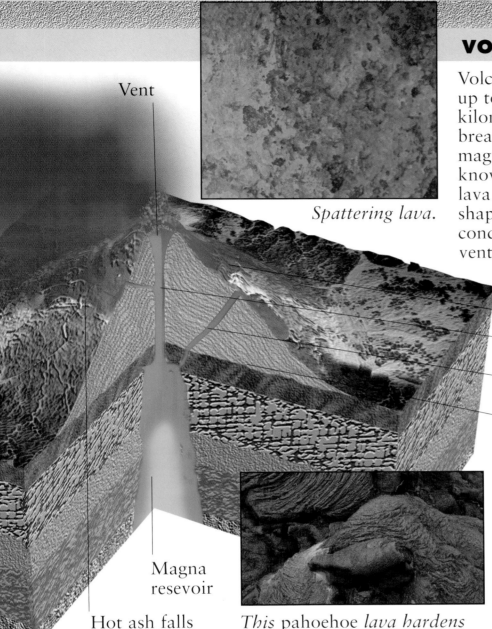

Vent

Spattering lava.

Lava flow

Main conduit

Secondary conduit

Layers of ash and lava form a cone

Magna reservoir

Hot ash falls on to slopes

This pahoehoe *lava hardens with a smooth surface.*

Olympus Mons

The Earth is not the only planet to have volcanoes. Olympus Mons, the largest volcano in the Solar System, is a giant volcano on the surface of Mars. It is 26 kilometres high and is thought to be extinct.

Olympus Mons on Mars.

VOLCANIC PLUGS

When a cone-shaped volcano stops erupting, what's left is a core of solidified magma, surrounded by a softer cone of ash and lava. The cone gradually wears away, leaving a column called a volcanic plug.

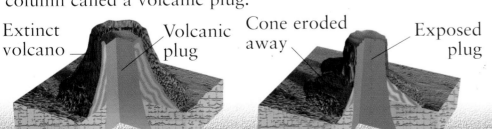

Extinct volcano

Volcanic plug

Cone eroded away

Exposed plug

There are thousands of volcanoes that we never see because they are hidden under the world's oceans. These volcanoes form huge mountain ranges under the water. Some are the tallest mountains on Earth.

HOT SPOTS

The biggest underwater volcanoes grow over places of high volcanic activity, called

hot spots. Here, magma breaks through the thin crust on the ocean floor. Tectonic plates move slowly, but hot spots stay still. As a plate moves over a hot spot, the hot spot creates a chain of volcanoes above.

In 1963 an undersea eruption created the island of Surtsey, near Iceland. Surtsey and Iceland are on top of the Mid-Atlantic spreading ridge.

SPREADING RIDGES

Underwater volcanoes also form where two tectonic plates move apart. Magma rises to fill the gap, creating fresh crust and ridges of mountains. This raised part of the ocean floor is called a spreading ridge. The Mid-Atlantic Ridge is a spreading ridge that stretches from Greenland to Antarctica.

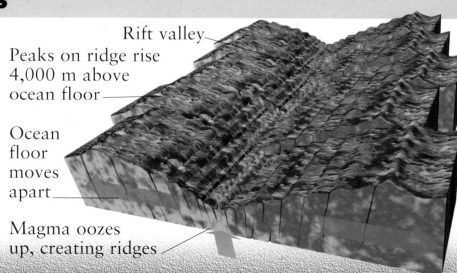

Rift valley

Peaks on ridge rise 4,000 m above ocean floor

Ocean floor moves apart

Magma oozes up, creating ridges

Sections move sideways along fractures called transform faults

Earth's tallest mountain

The Hawaiian Islands are the tops of a chain of underwater volcanoes. The summit of the extinct volcano of Mauna Kea, on the island of Hawaii, is 10,203 metres above the sea bed. This makes Mauna Kea the tallest mountain in the world. Mauna Loa, also in Hawaii, is the tallest active volcano.

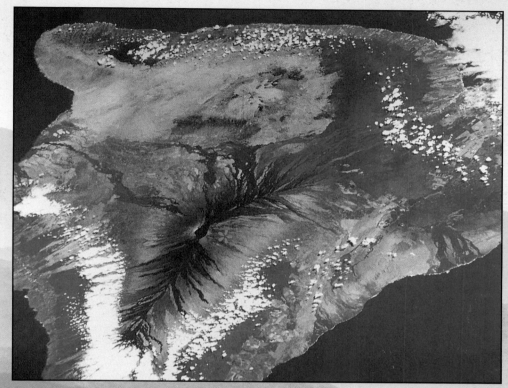

Hawaii. Mauna Kea is the dark shape at the bottom*.

Most underwater volcanoes are invisible, but some grow tall enough to break the water's surface, forming volcanic islands. Lava flows into the sea, creating plumes of steam as the hot rock makes the sea water boil.

Coral atolls are horseshoe-shaped islands made from coral reefs. Reefs are made from the hard skeletons of sea creatures called corals. They originally grew around the shorelines of volcanic islands. The volcanoes stopped erupting and collapsed into the sea, leaving the growing reef behind.

15

Howling winds, freezing temperatures, swirling clouds, storms and blizzards, and a covering of snow and ice, make mountain tops harsh places to be. This severe weather slowly breaks up solid rock, gradually wearing mountains down.

Jagged peaks like these in the High Sierra, California, USA, are caused by severe erosion.

WEATHER AND EROSION

Changes in temperature break up rocks on mountain tops. Rocks heat up in the sunshine, then cool quickly at night. Constant heating and cooling makes them crack. Sunshine also melts snow and ice. The water trickles into cracks in the rocks, then freezes at night. Because water expands slightly when it freezes, it widens the cracks. Rock fragments are carried away by wind and flowing water. This process is called erosion.

Broken pieces of rock called scree tumble down the mountain sides, creating slippery rocky slopes.

Rock fragments in fast-flowing mountain rivers erode the land into deep gorges, such as the Grand Canyon, Arizona, USA.

Kilimanjaro is a huge volcano in Tanzania. Although it is near the Equator and is surrounded by hot grasslands, the summit, at 5,895 metres, is always snow-capped.

Ötzi the iceman

In 1991 two climbers discovered a well-preserved body lying in a glacier in the Alps. Further scientific investigation revealed that the man had died about 5,000 years ago. He was probably killed by an arrow. Scientists named him Ötzi, after the valley where he was found.

Ötzi.

GLACIERS

A glacier is a slow-flowing river of ice. Glaciers start on mountain tops when deep layers of ice begin to slide downhill by a few centimetres a day. Boulders dragged along by the ice gouge U-shaped valleys in the mountain sides. Lower down the mountain, where the temperature is higher, the glacier melts.

Glacier

Lake filled with meltwater from ice caves under the glacier

Retreating glacier leaves a U-shaped valley dotted with smooth egg-shaped hills called drumlins

Medial moraine (rock fragments) collects on the edges of the glacier

Hanging valley formed from a tributary glacier

17

At 8,848 metres, Mount Everest is the world's highest mountain. It stands on the border between Nepal and Tibet, in the eastern Himalayas.

CLIMBING EVEREST

A successful attempt at climbing Everest requires careful planning, tonnes of equipment, good mountaineering skills, hard physical work, and luck with the weather. It takes several days to climb to the summit from base camp.

Mountaineers need warm, windproof clothes, boots with spikes called crampons, ice axes, ropes, food, fuel, tents, and even ladders. Goggles prevent glare from the snow which can cause snow blindness (inset below). Local people, called Sherpas, who are used to working in the thin mountain air, help to carry equipment to base camp (inset below right).

Climbers make camp several times on the way up Everest. High-altitude camps are often on rocky ledges. Tents, equipment and climbers are tied to the rock to stop them blowing away.

Sunset at Everest camp 2.

EVEREST THE MOUNTAIN

Everest is named after Sir George Everest (1790–1866), who was the first man to measure its height. Its local name is Chomolungma, which means Mother Goddess of the World. Everest is a jagged mountain. Sharp ridges with steep cliffs on either side lead to the summit. Its loose rocks and scree slopes are covered with snow and ice. Glaciers flow from its slopes into the valleys below. At the summit, the wind can blow at more than 200 km/h.

Everest viewed from the Tibetan foothills.

19

Everest conquered

The first attempts to climb Everest were made in the 1920s. Two British climbers, George Mallory and Andrew Irvine, died on Everest in 1924. Nobody knows if they reached the summit before they perished. The first successful climbers were New Zealander Edmund Hillary and Tenzing Norgay, a Sherpa from Nepal. They reached the top in 1953. Since then hundreds of climbers have climbed Everest by various routes. Many others have died trying.

Tenzing on the summit of Everest.

Animals that live in the mountains are adapted for the intense cold, strong winds and deep snow. Despite the harsh conditions, all sort of animals, from tiny insects to large mammals, survive here.

ADAPTING TO THE COLD

Mountain animals have different ways of coping with the cold. Mammals have very thick fur to stop precious body heat escaping. Some mammals, such as bears, hibernate when the winter snows arrive. Others move to the lower slopes to avoid the worst of the winter weather.

Llamas live high in the Andes, where the air is very thin. They have large lungs and hearts to compensate for the lack of oxygen.

Lynx.

Several species of cats, including the mountain lion (also called the cougar or puma) and the lynx hunt high in the mountains.

Mountain lion.

Wolves live in mountainous areas of the northern hemisphere, hunting anything from moose and deer to rabbits. They often hunt in packs.

These macaques live in Japan's mountains. In winter they warm up by bathing in hot volcanic springs.

Ibex – wild Asian mountain goats.

Yak

The yak is a species of cattle that lives at altitudes of up to 6,000 metres in the Himalayas, higher than any other mammal. It survives by eating the scarce tufty grass.

Yaks in a Himalayan valley.

Mountain goats.

Bighorn sheep.

Mountain goats and sheep live on steep mountain sides, and survive on grass. Goats escape from predators by moving along narrow ledges among the steep cliffs. Bighorn sheep have elastic pads on their feet to grip as they leap from rock to rock.

Plants that grow high up in the mountains must cope not only with the cold and wind, but also with the lack of water and soil. Like mountain animals, they have adapted to survive in unfavourable conditions.

FINDING A FOOTHOLD

Mountain plants have thin but strong roots that grow into cracks in the rocks. This anchors the plant to the mountain, stopping it from blowing away. Finding liquid water is a problem. The Alpine snowbell creates heat to melt surrounding snow.

Alpine plants such as the Edelweiss have furry leaves that trap heat from the Sun. The shape of the leaves also prevents precious water being lost by evaporation.

PLANT ZONES

As you move up the mountain slopes from the valley to the summit, the temperature drops, the wind increases, and the vegetation changes. Low down it is warm enough for deciduous trees. Further up, only conifers can grow. Higher still, no trees can survive at all, but there are meadows of grasses and alpine flowers. Above the meadows the ground is often frozen. Only hardy mosses, lichens and tiny plants can survive here. There is no life in the summit zone.

The level above which trees cannot survive is called the tree line.

RAIN SHADOWS

A wide variety of trees and shrubs grow in the world's mountains. In the tropics, lush forests thrive on the lower slopes. In colder climates, there are conifer forests and tough deciduous trees that grow close to the ground.

Mountain rainforests, or cloud forests, grow where a range of mountains creates a barrier to the weather. Damp air rises up the slopes and cools, forcing the moisture to fall as rain.

In Iceland's mountains, willow and birch trees, known as 'elfin wood', grow only a few centimetres high to keep out of the wind. Lichens survive by slowly dissolving the rocks to get nutrients.

Giant plants

The majority of high-altitude mountain plants are small and low to the ground. Two bizarre exceptions are the giant groundsels and giant lobelias that grow on the slopes of Mount Kenya in Africa. These amazing plants grow up to 10 metres high.

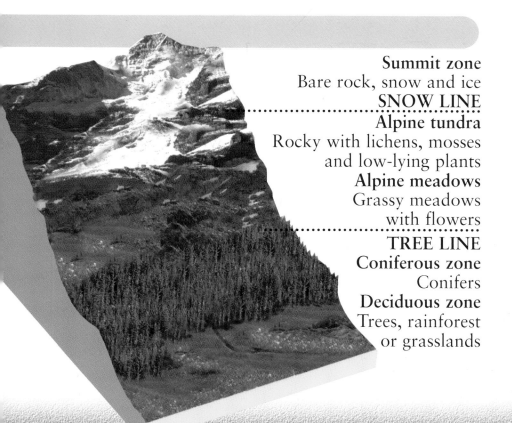

Summit zone
Bare rock, snow and ice
SNOW LINE
Alpine tundra
Rocky with lichens, mosses and low-lying plants
Alpine meadows
Grassy meadows with flowers
TREE LINE
Coniferous zone
Conifers
Deciduous zone
Trees, rainforest or grasslands

Giant groundsels.

23

About one in ten people in the world (about 500 million people in total) live in mountainous regions or near volcanoes. Like mountain plants and animals, they have found ways of surviving in the cold, the wind and the snow, and of farming the steep mountain slopes.

Sherpas are people of Tibetan descent who live in the southern foothills of the Himalayas in Nepal. They live by growing crops and keeping animals. Most Sherpas are extremely fit, and can carry heavy loads up long, steep hills for hours on end. That is why they work as porters on mountaineering expeditions.

The Aymara people fish on Lake Titicaca, 3,810 metres up in the Andes, on the borders of Bolivia and Peru. Their boats are made from the reeds that grow around the lake edge.

The highest city

The highest city in the world is Lhasa, the capital of Tibet, a region of China. Lhasa stands in a valley 3,660 metres above sea level, and is surrounded by the mountains of the Himalayas. Its most famous landmark is the spectacular Potala Palace.

Lhasa.

These terraced fields in the Andes were built more than 500 years ago by the Inca people. They are still in use. Each one is supported by a stone wall.

The Indian people of Ecuador have extra numbers of red blood cells to carry oxygen around their bodies, to cope with the thin air at high altitude.

MOUNTAIN FARMING

Most mountain peoples make a living by growing crops such as potatoes and maize, and raising animals, such as sheep and llamas. Farmers create flat fields by building terraces on the steep hillsides. The terraces stop the soil from washing away and trap precious water. Animals are moved to high mountain pastures in spring and summer. Larger animals such as llamas are used for transport. Animal hair is also woven and knitted into clothes and carpets.

25

One of the greatest dangers to people who live, work and play in the mountains is the avalanche. An avalanche happens when thousands of tonnes of snow suddenly slips down the side of a mountain.

AVALANCHE DANGERS

Avalanches can travel at more than 300 kilometres per hour. When they stop, the snow sets hard, making it almost impossible for anybody trapped under the snow to escape. Skiers and mountaineers can set off avalanches if they ski or walk across snow slopes. Even a very loud noise can trigger an avalanche.

HOW AVALANCHES HAPPEN

An avalanche happens when the layers of snow on a slope become loose. A slab avalanche starts when a slab of snow breaks away and begins to slide over a weak layer of snow underneath.

On very steep slopes like these cliffs on Everest, a small avalanche can set off more avalanches underneath. This is called a loose avalanche.

In 1999, after days of heavy snowfall, an avalanche hit the Austrian village of Galtur, killing 31 people. Anti-avalanche fences would have given some protection.

Testing for avalanches

Scientists try to predict when avalanches are likely to happen so that warnings can be given. They analyse data from weather stations, and check out the snow slopes. Sometimes they set off avalanches on purpose to clear a dangerously overloaded slope.

The chances of surviving an avalanche are quite good if you are found quickly. Rescuers search for victims with sniffer dogs and long poles that they push into the snow.

Examining snow layers on a slope.

As well as being the homes of plants, animals and people, mountains are an important resource for industries and tourism. Unfortunately, some human activities scar the mountains. Many mountain ranges have been made into national parks to protect them.

METAL, MINERALS AND WOOD

Metals, minerals and timber are precious mountain resources. Rocks contain gemstones and metal ores that contain gold, silver, copper and other metals. Cutting down mountain forests for their wood allows erosion to start, creating bare slopes and mud slides.

Skiing is the most popular mountain sport of all. Most skiers stay in purpose-built resorts and ski on prepared runs called pistes. Off-piste skiing is exciting but it can be dangerous because of sharp drops and avalanches.

A type of gas-filled volcanic stone called pumice is mined here. People use pumice stone to smooth rough skin.

MOUNTAIN LEISURE

Spectacular mountains and volcanoes are popular tourist destinations. Roads, railways and cable cars carry visitors to their summits. Mountain sports include skiing, hiking, rock climbing, mountaineering, rafting and paragliding. All these activities can spoil the mountain environment. Recently a programme has begun to clear Everest of the many tonnes of rubbish left behind by mountaineers.

Abseiling is a quick way of descending after a climb.

Hydroelectric power station.

Power from the mountains

High rainfall, melting snows, powerful rivers and steep-sided valleys combine to make mountains ideal sites for water-supply reservoirs and hydroelectric power stations. Water is trapped in a reservoir by building a concrete dam between the valley sides. It is allowed to flow down pipes to a power station. Here, it turns turbines, which turn generators that produce electricity.

29

THE HIGHEST MOUNTAIN	At 8,848 metres, Mount Everest, on the borders of Nepal and Tibet in the Himalayas, is the world's highest mountain. The world's fourth highest mountain, Lhotse (8,501 metres), is just 5 kilometres away along a rocky ridge. Second and third highest are K2 (8,611 metres) and Kanchenjunga (8,598 metres), also in the Himalayas.
THE HIGHEST MOUNTAIN RANGE	The Himalayas, in central Asia, is the highest mountain range. It stretches 2,600 kilometres across the top of India. Nine of the world's highest mountains, all more than 8,000 metres high, are in the Himalayas. The remaining one, K2, is in the neighbouring Karakoram range.
THE LONGEST MOUNTAIN RANGE	The Andes on the western edge of South America is the world's longest mountain range. It stretches 7,250 kilometres from Venezuela in the north to the southern tip of Chile. The highest peak in the Andes is Aconcagua (6,960 metres).
WORLD RECORDS	The highest mountains in each continent are: North America: Mount McKinley, USA (6,194 metres). South America: Aconcagua, Argentina (6,960 metres). Europe: Mont Blanc, France/Italy (4,807 metres). Africa: Kilimanjaro, Tanzania (5,895 metres). Asia: Mount Everest, Nepal/Tibet (8,848 metres). Australasia: Jaya, Indonesia (5,030 metres). Antarctica: Mount Erebus (3,794 metres).
THE HIGHEST VOLCANO	All of the world's highest volcanoes are in the Andes. The highest active volcano in the world, above sea level, is Guallatiri, in Chile, at 6,060 metres. Llullaillaco (6,739 metres), also in Chile, is higher, but dormant.
THE MOST ACTIVE VOLCANO	Kilauea, on the island of Hawaii, is the world's most active volcano. It has been erupting continuously since 1983. Hawaii holds other volcano records, too. Measured from the ocean floor (rather than from sea level), Mauna Loa is the world's highest active volcano, and Mauna Kea is the world's highest mountain.
THE LONGEST GLACIER	The longest glacier in the world is the Lambert-Fisher glacier in Antarctica. It flows 515 kilometres from the Antarctic plateau, more than 3,000 metres up, down to the sea.

GLOSSARY

active
Describes a volcano that erupts continuously or very regularly.

conifer
A large, often pyramid-shaped tree that grows cones and needle-shaped leaves, such as pine trees, spruce and larches. Most conifers are evergreens.

crust
The layer of solid rock that forms the outer layer of the Earth.

deciduous
Describes trees that lose their leaves in autumn and grow new ones in spring. This reduces the amount of water they lose by evaporation.

dormant
Describes a volcano that has not erupted for many years.

evaporation
The process of water turning to vapour in the air when it is heated.

glacier
A river of ice that flows very slowly down the side of a mountain, eroding the land into a U-shaped valley.

magma
Hot, molten rock beneath the Earth's crust. Magma that leaks out from under the crust is called lava.

ore
A mineral that contains a metal. A metal is taken out of its ore using heat or chemicals.

pahoehoe
Very runny lava that cools to form smooth, folded mounds of rock. A thin skin forms on *pahoehoe* lava as it cools, but the lava continues to flow underneath. *Aa* is thicker lava than *pahoehoe*, which cools to form jagged chunks of rock.

tectonic plate
A huge section of the Earth's crust. The crust is broken into several tectonic plates.